samsoon adventures 🦋

samsoon adventures 🍀

samsoon adventures ✿

Spring, Summer with Samsoon

samsoon adventures 🐾

samsoon adventures 🐾

Author's Note

Hello!

I am grateful to share Samsoon along
with your Korean learning adventure.

The workbook involves practicing Korean words (Hangul)
and coloring Samsoon Adventures illustrations.

I hope the coloring adds a place of solitude to take breaks
between your Korean learning exercises.

I want to thank and acknowledge my mother,
who encouraged me ever since I could grab a pencil
and have dreams of my own.

I hope the Samsoon Adventures workbook motivates your learning process,
like how my mother encouraged me at every step of my creative flow.

Dream on!
With love & light,
 Soon Ju & mother

samsoon adventures 🌸

samsoon adventures 🎀

samsoon adventures 🐾

samsoon adventures 🐾

samsoon adventures ✿

Dedicated to

samsoon adventures 🏵️

samsoon adventures 🐾

봄

1 - 1

samsoon adventures ✿

스포츠

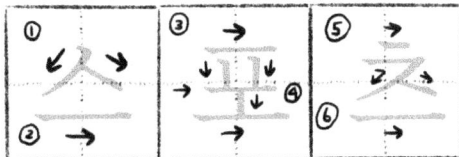

(s-por-tes)

sports

점프

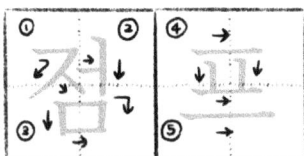

(ju-ump)

jump

봄

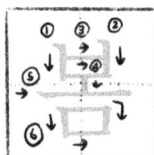

(bom)

spring

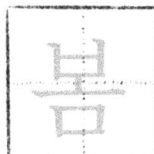

연필

연 필

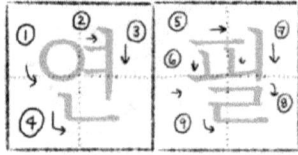

(yun-pil)
pencil

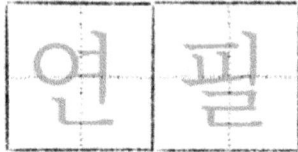

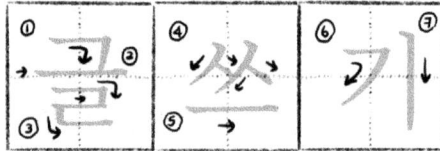

연 필

글쓰기

글 쓰 기

(gul-suh-gi)
writing

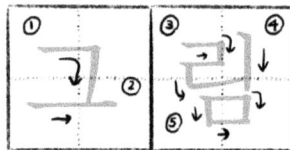

글 쓰 기

그림

그 림

(guh-rim)
drawing

그 림

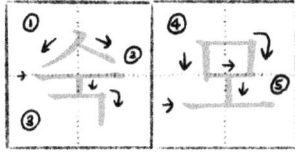

숙모

숙 모 (suk-moh)
aunt

숙 모

우정

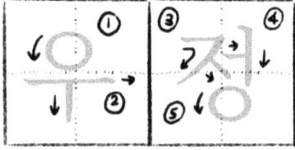

우 정 (ooh-jung)
friendship

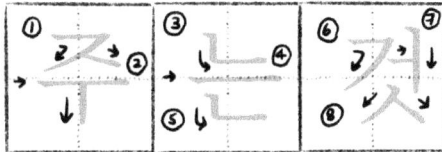

우 정

주는것

주 는 것 (joo-neun-gut)
giving

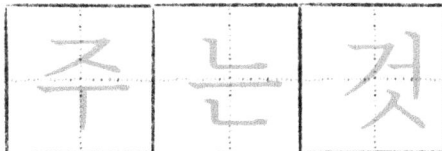

주 는 것

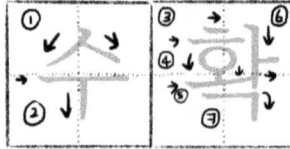

(soo-hwak)

harvest

수 확

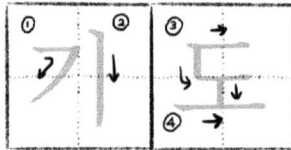

(gi-doh)

pray

기 도

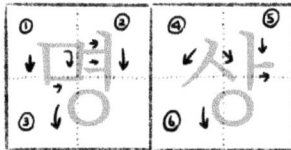

(myung-sang)

meditation

명 상

samsoon adventures 🌸

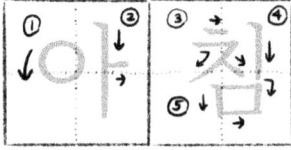

아침 (ah-chim)
morning

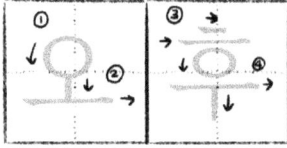

오후 (oh-hoo)
afternoon

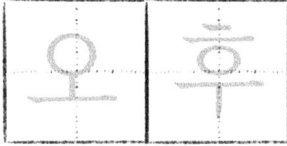

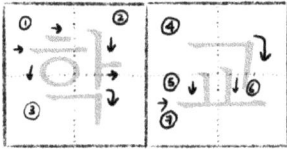

학교 (Hak-gyo)
school

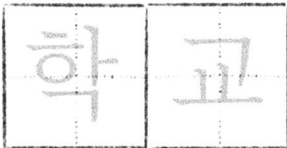

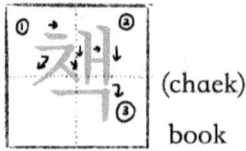 (chaek)

book

책

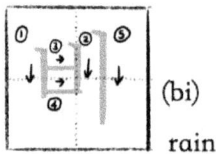 (bi)

rain

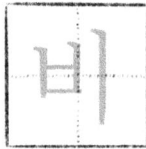

비

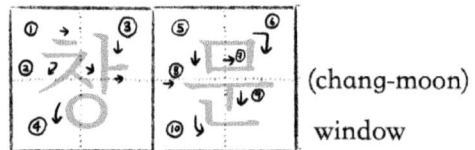 (chang-moon)

window

창문

우산

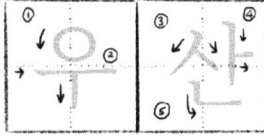

(ooh-san)

umbrella

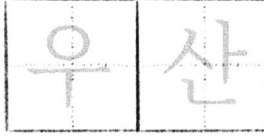

해바라기

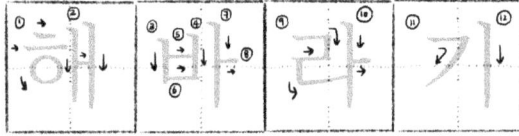

(hae-ba-ra-gi)

sunflower

꽃

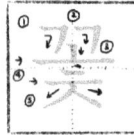

(kkot)

flower

samsoon adventures

초록

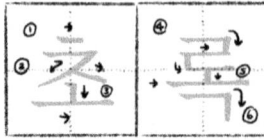

(cho-rok)

green

노랑

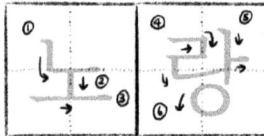

(noh-rang)

yellow

주황

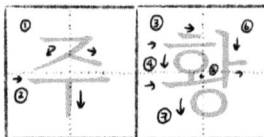

(joo-hwang)

orange

분홍

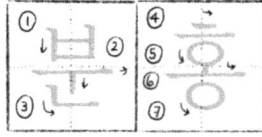

(boon-hong)

pink

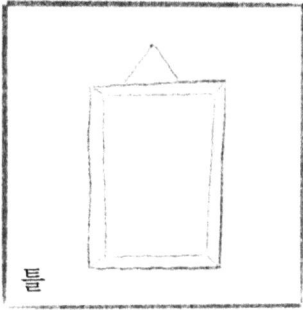

틀

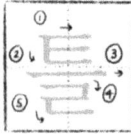

(teul)

frame

그림

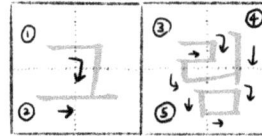

(geuh-rim)

painting

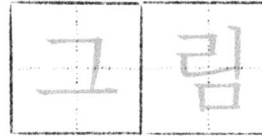

머리핀

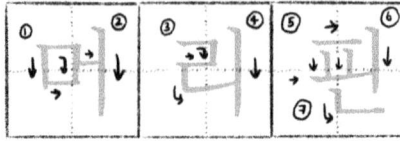

(muh-ri-pin)

hairpin

바구니

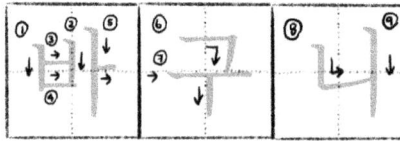
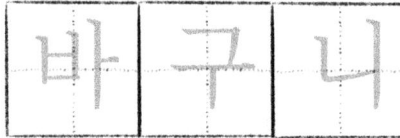

(bah-goo-ni)

basket

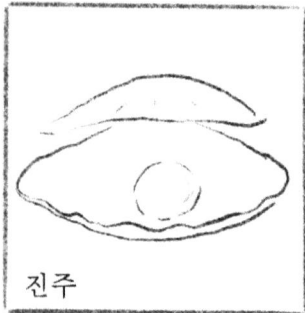

진주

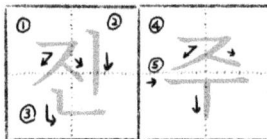
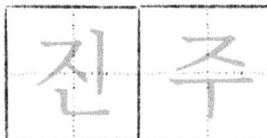

(jin-joo)

pearl

빙수

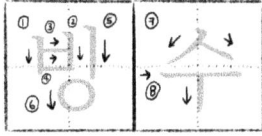

빙 수 (bing-soo)
shaved ice

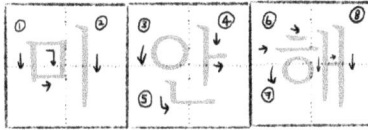

빙 수

미안해

미 안 해 (mi-ahn-hae)
sorry

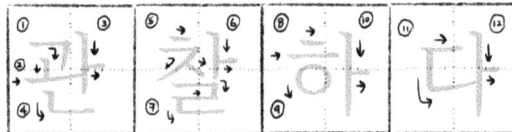

미 안 해

관찰하다

관 찰 하 다 (kwan-chal-ha-da)
observe

관 찰 하 다

고양이

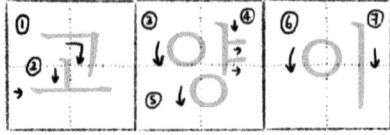

(go-yaang-ee)

cat

물고기

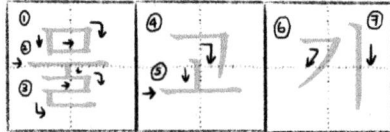

(mul-go-gi)

fish

거북이

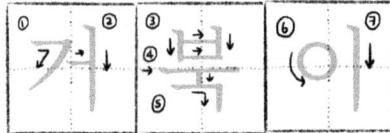

(guh-book-ee)

turtle

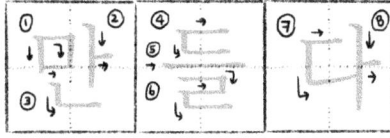

만들다 (man-deul-dah)
making

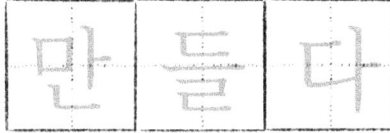

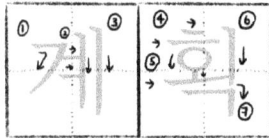

만 들 다

계획 (gye-hwaek)
plan

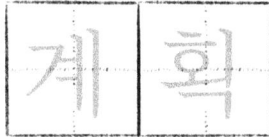

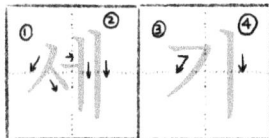

계 획

세기 (sae-gi)
counting

세 기

달 걀 (dal-gyal)

egg

달 걀

새 둥 지 (sae-doong-ji)

bird's nest

새 둥 지

개 구 리 (gae-goo-ri)

frog

개 구 리

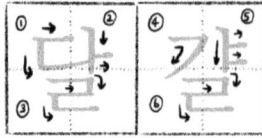

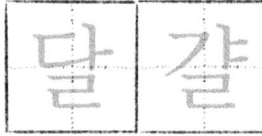

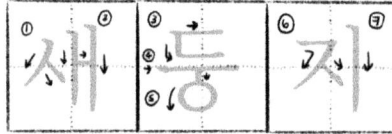

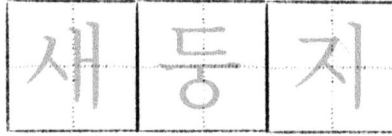

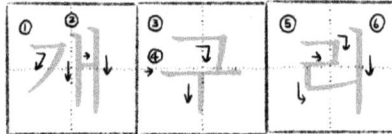

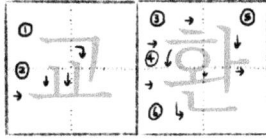

(gyo-hwan)

exchange

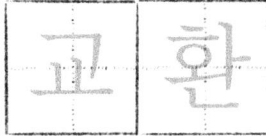

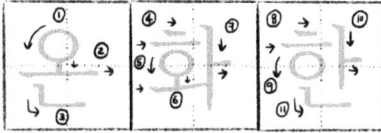

(own-hwa-han)

gentle

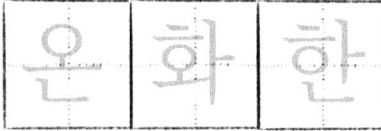

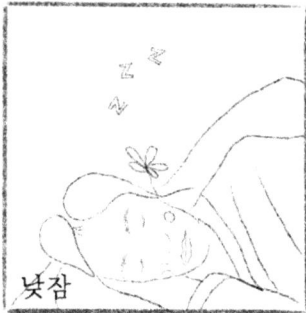

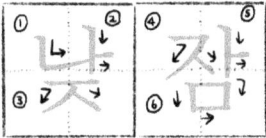

(nat-jam)

nap

공기

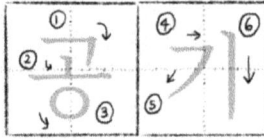

(gong-gi)

air

지구

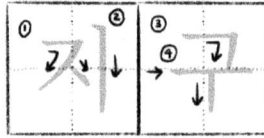

(ji-goo)

earth

호흡

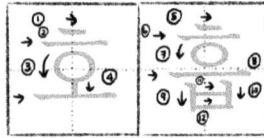

(hoh-heup)

breathing

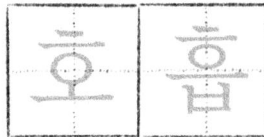

예술

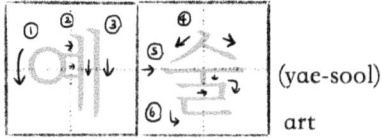

(yae-sool)

art

예 술

장식

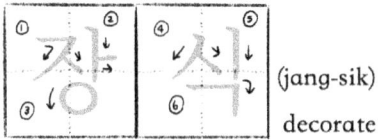

(jang-sik)

decorate

장 식

찻집

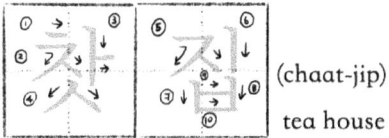

(chaat-jip)

tea house

찻 집

samsoon adventures 🐾

samsoon adventures 🦋

samsoon adventures

samsoon adventures ✿

samsoon adventures ✿

samsoon adventures

samsoon adventures 🍀

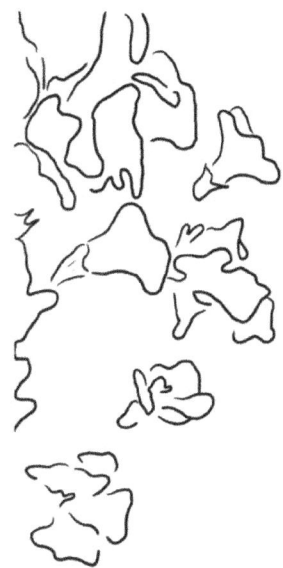

samsoon adventures 🌼

samsoon adventures

samsoon adventures

samsoon adventures ❀

samsoon adventures ❀

여름

1 - 2

여름

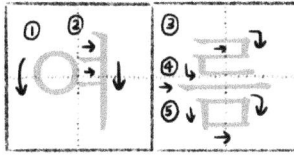 (yuh-reum)
summer

해변

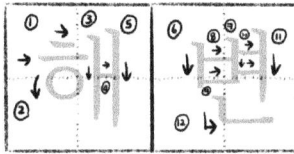 (hae-byeun)
beach

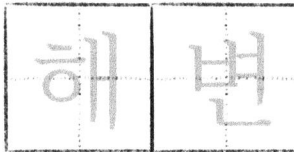

부산

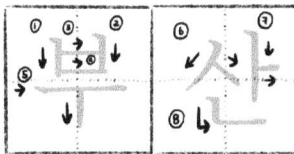 (boo-san)
Busan

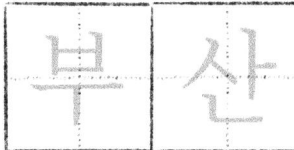

samsoon adventures ✿

하이킹

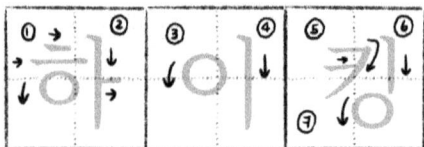

(hah-ee-king)
hiking

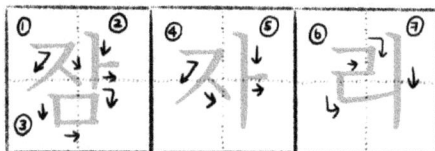

잠자리

(jam-ja-ree)
dragonfly

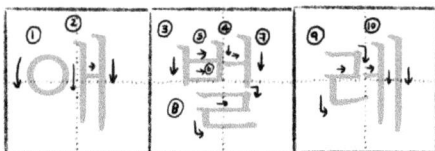

애벌레

(ae-bul-rae)
caterpillar

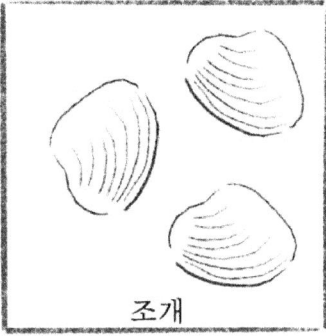

조개

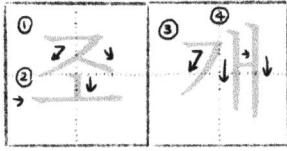
(jo-gae)

clam

거품

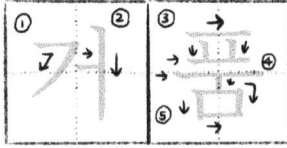
(guh-poom)

foam

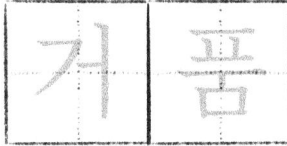

가족

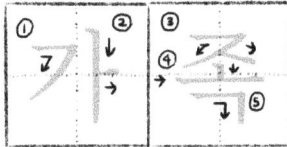
(gah-jok)

family

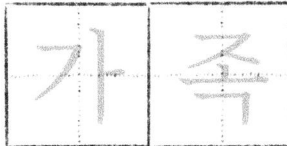

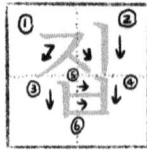

집 (jip)
house

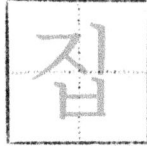

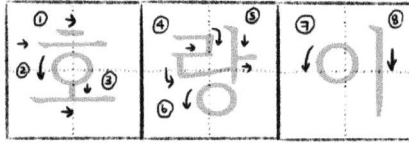

호랑이 (ho-rang-ee)
tiger

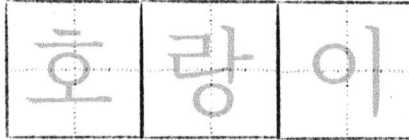

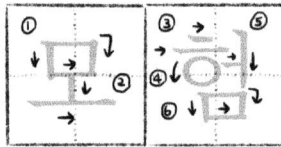

모험 (moh-hum)
adventure

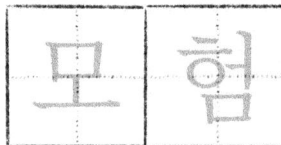

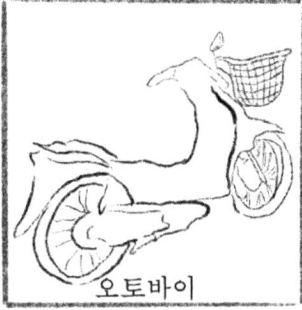

오토바이

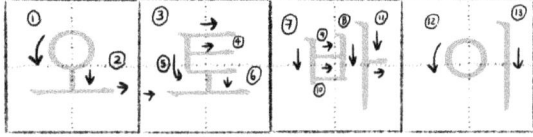

(o-to-bah-ee)

motorcycle

오 토 바 이

구름

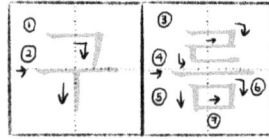

(goo-reum)

cloud

구 름

옛날

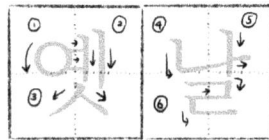

(yaet-nal)

long ago

옛 날

수박

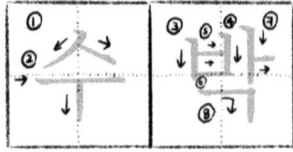

(soo-bak)

watermelon

옥수수

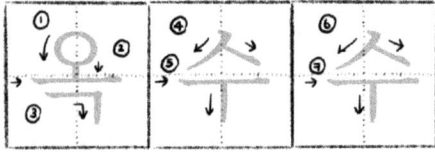

(ohk-soo-soo)

corn

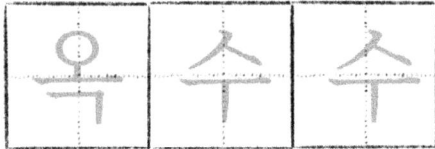

귤

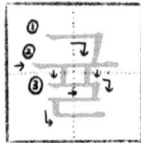

(gyeul)

tangerine

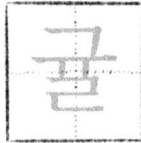

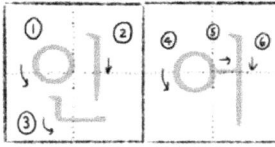

안어

인 어 (in-uh)
mermaid

인 어

발자국

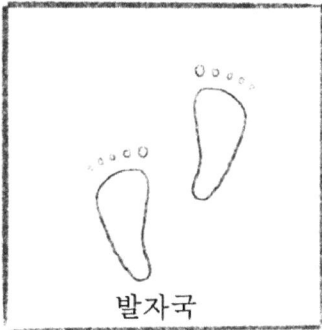

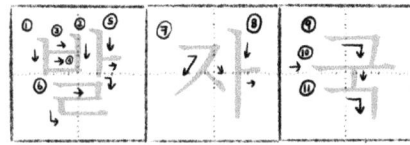

발 자 국 (bal-jah-ghook)
footprint

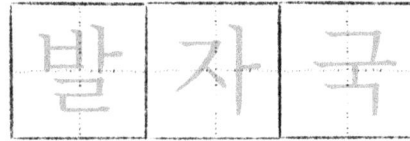

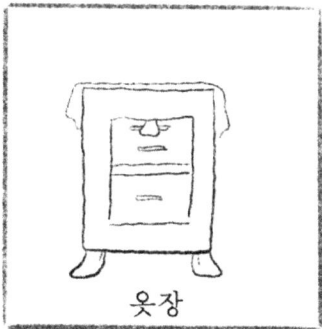

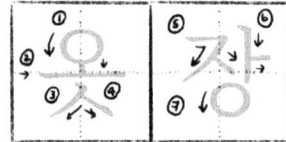

발 자 국

옷장

옷 장 (oht-jang)
dresser

옷 장

물방울

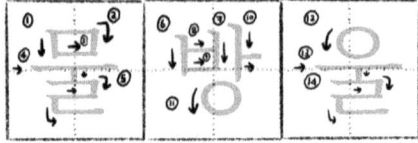

물방울 (mool-bang-eul)
bubble

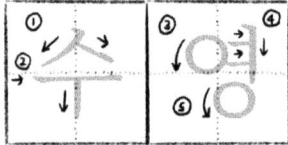

물방울

수영 (sooh-yeung)
swim

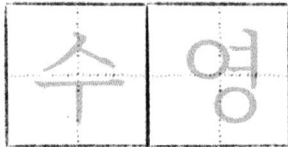

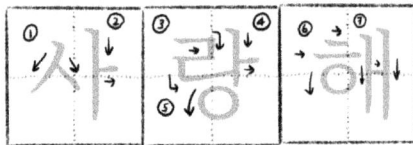

수영

사랑해 (sah-rang-hae)
love you

사랑해

목소리

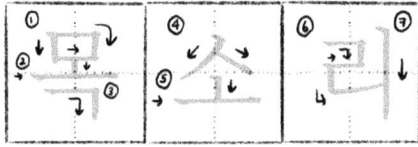

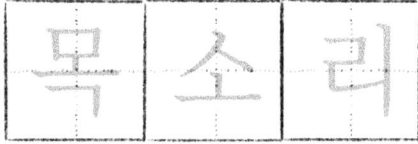

목 소 리 (mok-so-ree)

voice

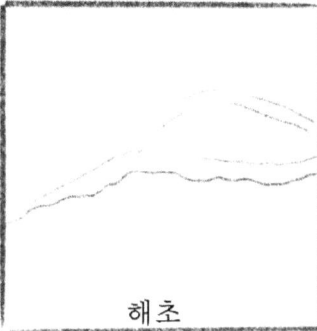

해초

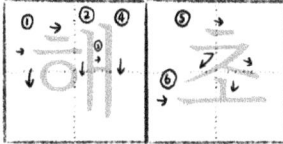

(hae-cho)

seaweed

모래

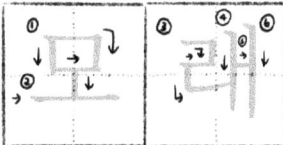

(moh-rae)

sand

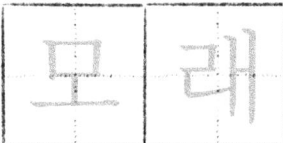

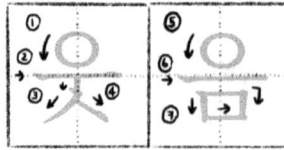

(oot-eum)

laughter

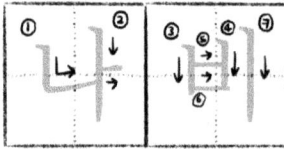

(nah-bee)

butterfly

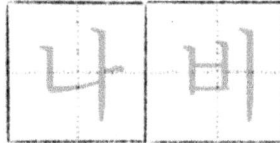

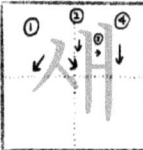

(sae)

bird

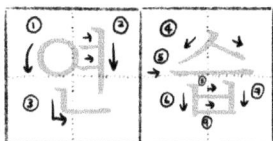 (yeun-seup)

practice

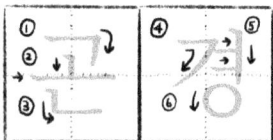 (gon-gyeung)

difficulty

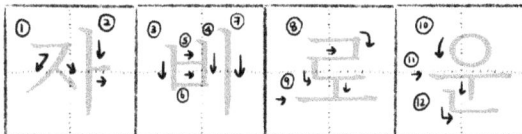 (jah-be-ro-eun)

generous

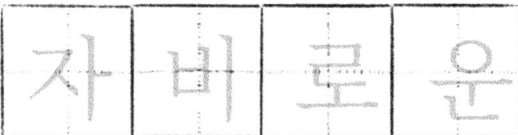

복숭아꽃

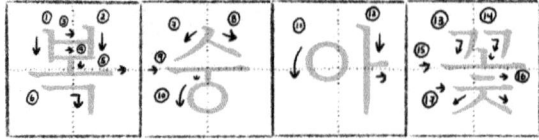

(bok-soong-a-kkot)

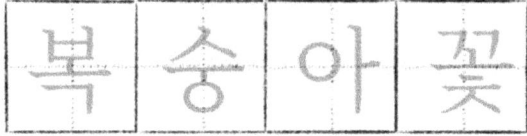

peach flower

복 숭 아 꽃

정원

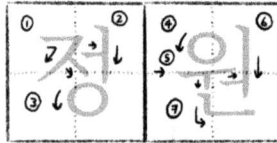

(jung-won)

garden

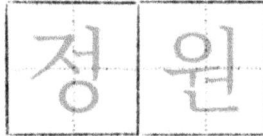

정 원

개울

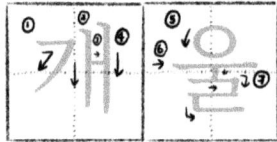

(gae-eul)

creek

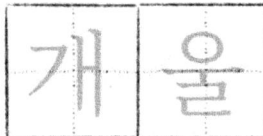

개 울

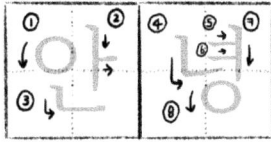

안 녕 (ahn-nyeung) hello

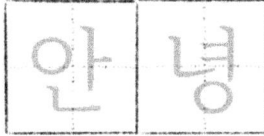

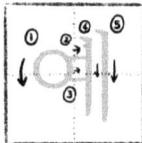

안 녕

예 (yae) yes

예

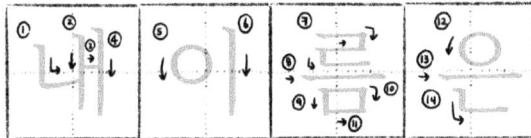

내 이 름 은 (nae-ee-reum-eun) my name is

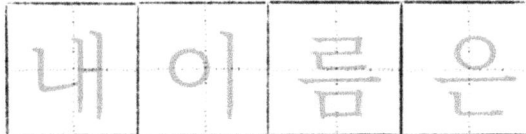

내 이 름 은

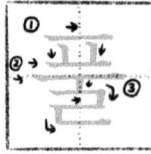

(pul)

grass

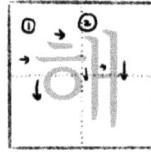

(hae)

sun

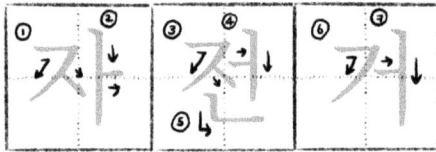

(jah-jeun-guh)

bicycle

모래성

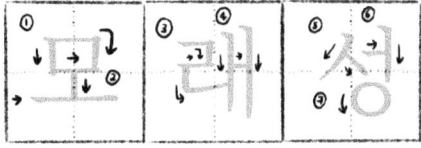

(moe-rae-sung)

sandcastle

바람

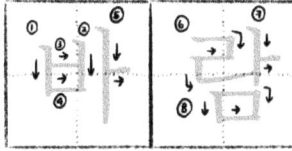

(bah-raam)

wind

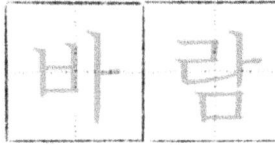

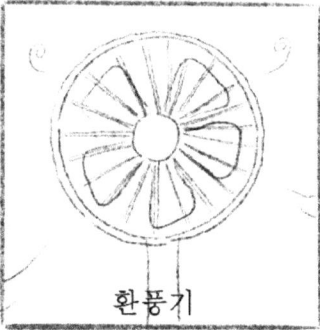

환풍기

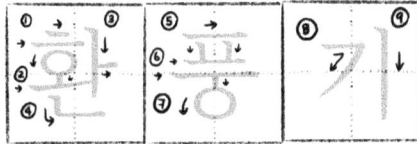

hwan-poong-gi)

fan

samsoon adventures 🍀

감상

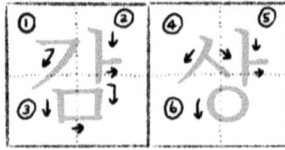

(gam-saang)

appreciate

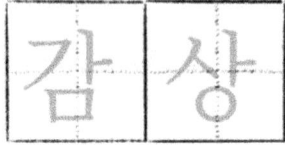

흙

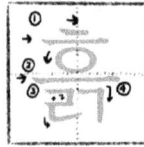

(heuk)

soil

캠핑

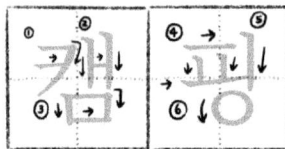

(cam-ping)

camping

 음악

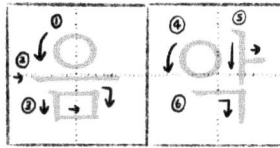 (eum-ahk)

music

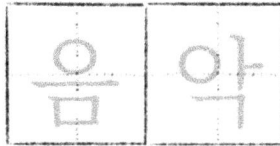

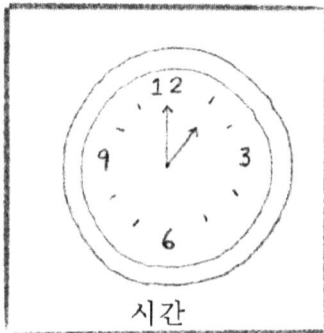 시간

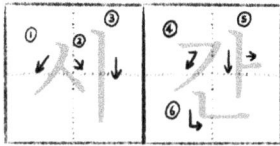 (si-gaan)

time

 미소

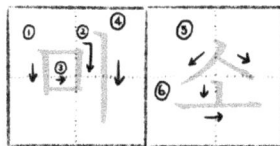 (mi-soh)

smile

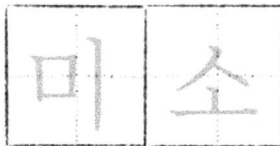

samsoon adventures ❀

samsoon adventures 🌸

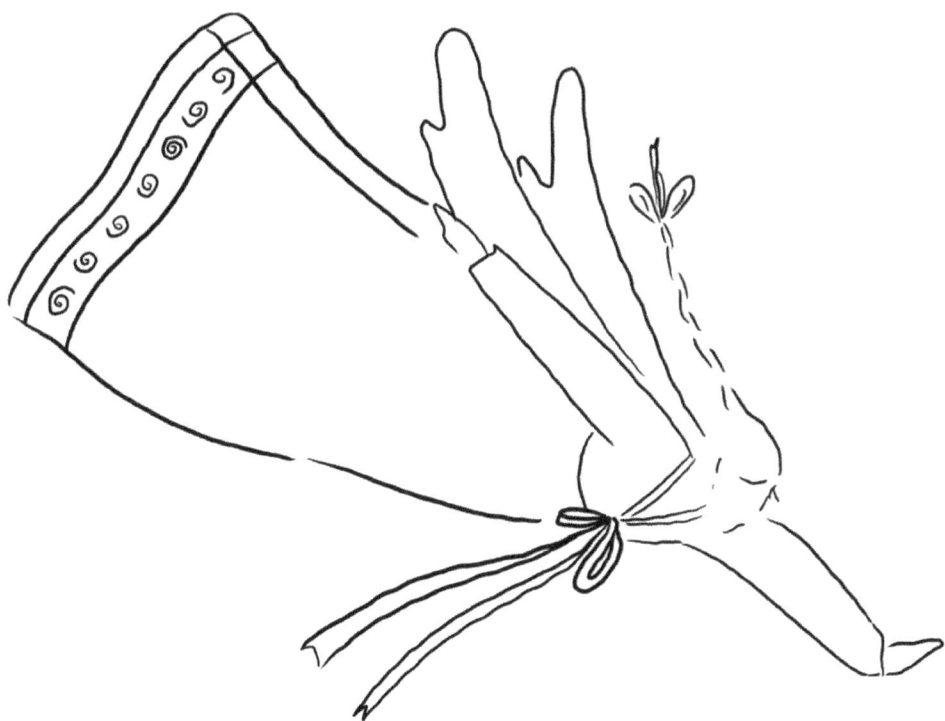

samsoon adventures 🌸

samsoon adventures

samsoon adventures 🍀

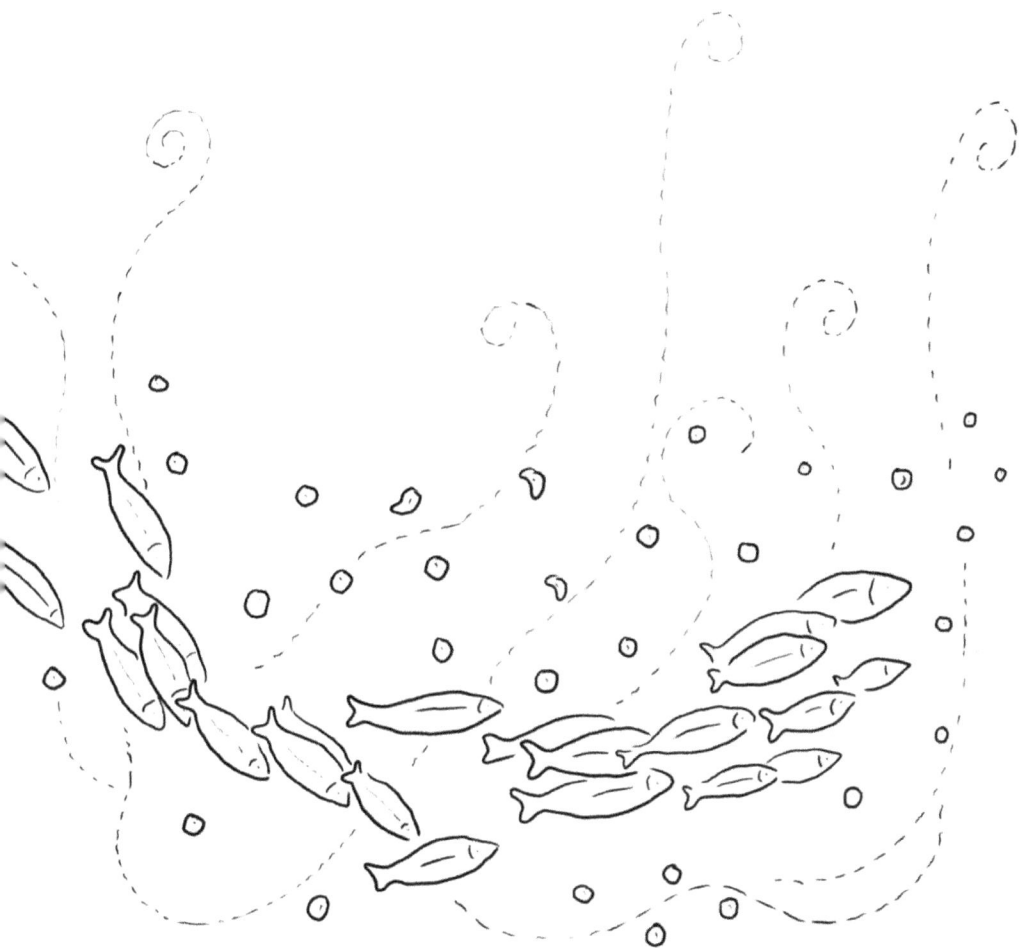

samsoon adventures 🐾

samsoon adventures 🍀

samsoon adventures

samsoon adventures 🐾

samsoon adventures ✿

Samsoon Adventures

Hangul with Samsoon

 Write your daily Korean sentences with a square-style notebook, suitable for all ages!

Recommended for beginners, with dotted squares inside.

Flowers with Samsoon

Immersive Korean self-learning flower exercises for all ages, with easy how-to-pronounce, how-to-write steps provided.

Samsoon Adventures

Another Day, Another Blessing

 Write down your self-guided, self-oriented daily to-dos, gratitude, and reflections.

Mindfulness productivity design inspired by Korean time wheel.

Cultivate an ever-blossoming self-purposeful garden! How-to use provided.

Samsoon
Adventures

Samsoon and Farewells

Written and illustrated by
Soon Ju Kim

Samsoon and Farewells

Samsoon and Mimi were best friends, finding joy in everyday experiences with their Grandma.

One day, Samsoon faces the reality of departing from her best friend.

We learn with Samsoon the beauty of departures and how to overcome them gracefully.

Samsoon Adbentures

www.ingramcontent.com/pod-product-compliance
Lightning Source LLC
Chambersburg PA
CBHW051433090426
42737CB00014B/2948